FRANCIS MARION

Swamp Fox of South Carolina

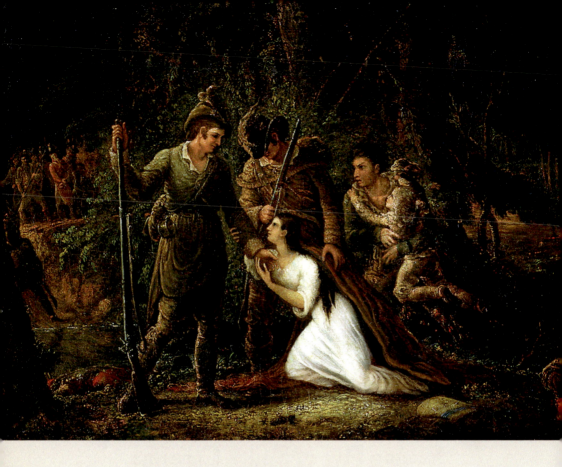

FORGOTTEN HEROES
OF THE AMERICAN REVOLUTION

Nathanael Greene: The General Who Saved the Revolution

Henry Knox: Washington's Artilleryman

Francis Marion: Swamp Fox of South Carolina

Daniel Morgan: Fighting Frontiersman

John Stark: Live Free or Die

FRANCIS MARION

Swamp Fox of South Carolina

Scott Kaufman

OTTN
PUBLISHING
STOCKTON, NJ

DEDICATION: To my grandmother, Ruth Kaufman.

Frontispiece: Two members of Francis Marion's militia comfort American prisoners they have just rescued from British soldiers. By using small bands of fast-moving soldiers to surprise their enemies, Marion's men were able to keep up the fighting in South Carolina long after other Americans had given up.

OTTN Publishing
16 Risler Street
Stockton, NJ 08859
www.ottnpublishing.com

Copyright © 2007 by OTTN Publishing. All rights reserved.
Printed and bound in the United States of America.

First printing

1 3 5 7 9 8 6 4 2

Library of Congress Cataloging-in-Publication Data

Kaufman, Scott.
  Francis Marion / Scott Kaufman.
      p. cm. — (Forgotten heroes of the American Revolution)
  Summary: "A biography of the Colonial leader who achieved notable successes
leading guerrilla forces against the British in South Carolina during the American
Revolution"—Provided by publisher.
  Includes bibliographical references and index.
  ISBN-13: 978-1-59556-014-8 (hc)
  ISBN-10: 1-59556-014-9 (hc)
  ISBN-13: 978-1-59556-019-3 (pb)
  ISBN-10: 1-59556-019-X (pb)
  1. Marion, Francis, 1732-1795—Juvenile literature. 2. Generals—United States—
Biography—Juvenile literature. 3. South Carolina—Militia—Biography—Juvenile
literature. 4. United States—History—Revolution, 1775-1783—Biography—Juve-
nile literature. 5. South Carolina—History—Revolution, 1775-1783—Juvenile lit-
erature. I. Title. II. Series.
  E207.M3K38 2006
  973.3'3092—dc22
                            2006000073

Publisher's Note: All quotations in this book come from original sources, and contain the spelling and grammatical inconsistencies of the original text.

TABLE OF CONTENTS

Why Francis Marion Should Be Remembered

"I am extreamly pleased with your managem't & success & resquest you earnestly to continue your Hostilities against our Tyrannic and cruel Enemies. . . . The Enemy may be much destracted and divided by your different attacks & the Country well covered by your Joint endeavors."

—Horatio Gates, letter to Francis Marion, October 11, 1780

"When I consider how much you have done and suffered, and under what disadvantage you have maintained your ground, I am at a loss which to admire most, your courage and fortitude, or your address and management. Certain it is no man has a better claim to the public thanks, or is more generally admired than you are. History affords no instance wherein an officer has kept possession of a country under so many disadvantages as you have; surrounded on every side with a superior force; hunted from every quarter with veteran troops, you have found means to elude all their attempts, and to keep alive the expiring hopes of an oppressed Militia, when all succour seemed to be cut off. To fight the enemy bravely with a prospect of victory is nothing; but to fight with intrepidity under the constant impression of a defeat, and inspire irregular troops to do it, is a talent peculiar to yourself."

—Nathanael Greene, letter to Francis Marion, April 1781

"He was reserved and silent, entering into conversation only when necessary, and then with modesty and good sense. He possessed a strong mind, improved by its own reflections and observations, not by books or travel. His dress was like his address— plain, regarding comfort and decency only. In his meals he was abstemious, eating generally of one dish, and drinking water mostly. He was sedulous and constant in his attention to the duties of his station, to which every other consideration yielded. Even the charms of the fair, like the luxuries of the table and the allurements of wealth, seemed to be lost upon him. The procurement of subsistence for his men, and the continuance of annoyance for his enemy, engrossed his entire mind. He was virtuous all over; never, even in manner, much less in reality, did he trench upon right. Beloved by his friends, and respected by his enemies, he exhibited a luminous example of the beneficial effects to be produced by an individual who, with only small means at his command, possesses a virtuous heart, a strong head, and a mind directed to the common good."

—Henry Lee, in *Memoirs of the War in the Southern Department* (1812)

"Resolved, That the thanks of the United States, in Congress assembled, be presented to Brigadier General Marion, of the South Carolina Militia, for his wise, gallant, and decided conduct, in defending the liberties of his country."

—Congress of the United States, October 29, 1781

"Your conduct merits the applause of your countrymen. Your courage, your vigilance, and your abilities have exceeded their most sanguine expectations, and have answered all their hopes. Whilst the virtue of gratitude shall form a part of our national character, your important services to this country can never be forgotten."

—President of the Senate of South Carolina, February 28, 1783

"We, citizens of the district of Georgetown, finding you no longer at our head, have agreed to convey to you our grateful sentiments for your former numerous services. . . . Our children shall hereafter point out the places and say to their children, here Gen. Marion, posted to advantage, made a glorious stand in defence of the liberties of his country; there, on disadvantageous ground, retreated to save the lives of his fellow citizens. What could be more glorious for the general commanding free men than thus to fight, and thus to save the lives of his fellow soldiers?"

—William James, address at Marion's retirement from the South Carolina militia in 1794

"Marion's hit-and-run tactics against the British during Cornwallis' advance into the South proved effective. . . . His attacks showed how a tiny band of skirmishers, who had the advantage of terrain on their side, could unhinge the operations of a much larger body of traditionally deployed troops, even troops who had been led to expect this type of attack."

—Historians John Keegan and Andrew Wheatcroft, in *Who's Who in Military History* (1996)

"As a classic guerrilla leader Marion's only peers in American history were such great native warriors as Osceola or Cochise. . . . Marion for the most part engaged in the stock-in-trade of guerrillas throughout the ages: ambushes and hit-and-run raids. He dispersed and disappeared when the odds were against him, and reappeared after his enemies announced that he had been driven from the field. . . . His attitude and actions were largely governed by the principle of cooperation. Overall the dark-visaged little genius . . . put the common cause ahead of himself."

—Historian John Buchanan, in *The Road to Guilford Courthouse* (1997)

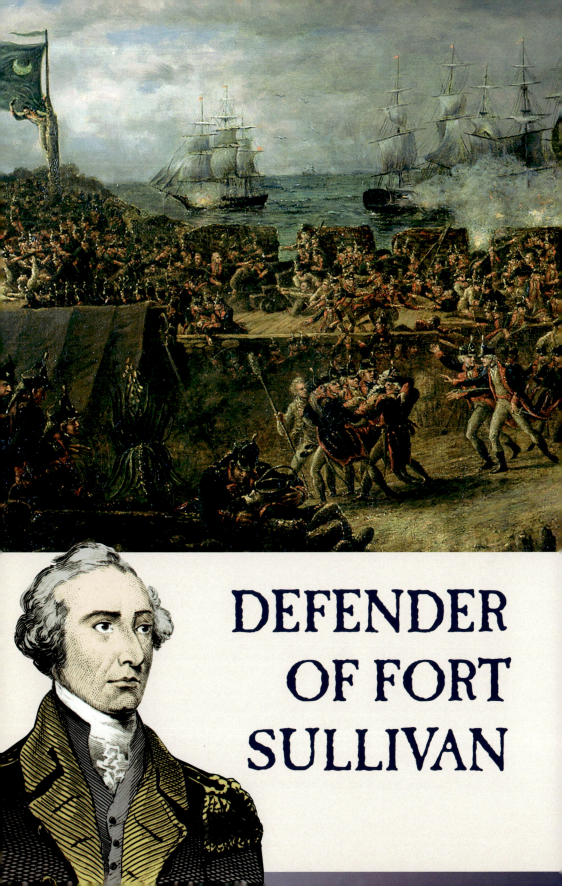

DEFENDER OF FORT SULLIVAN

Francis Marion (opposite, bottom) was a 44-year-old major in the South Carolina militia when a British fleet arrived at Charleston in June 1776. Although the defenders were outnumbered, they successfully fought off the British naval attack. In this painting of the attack on Fort Sullivan, Marion and other officers are pictured at lower right conferring with their commander, William Moultrie.

1

"A fleet, a fleet, ho!" shouted a lookout, as British ships sailed into view of Sullivan's Island. It was June 1776, and the American soldiers defending Charleston, South Carolina, had been expecting an attack for months. Charleston was among the most important seaports in the 13 American colonies. If the British captured the port, they could flood the southern colonies with soldiers and supplies, and squash the spreading rebellion there.

The revolt against British rule had begun in the spring of 1775, when colonists in Massachusetts clashed with British troops at Lexington and Concord. Many Americans had been angry about British government policies for a long time, so the *insurrection* soon spread to the other colonies.

DIVIDE AND CONQUER

In 1776, General William Howe, the commander of British forces in North America, devised a plan to divide and conquer the rebels. Howe and other British leaders believed that the desire for independence was strongest in northern colonies like Massachusetts and New York, but that most people in the southern colonies would remain loyal to the king. Howe planned to send a small army to stamp out the rebellion in the South, expecting *Loyalists* to support the British troops. His main force would be sent to capture New York. This would cut off Massachusetts from the rest of the colonies, and make it easy to defeat the rebels in the north.

Taking the South was supposed to be the easy part of the plan. But by the time the British fleet arrived at Charleston, Loyalist forces in South Carolina had already been defeated. Instead of finding supporters, the British found a small group of *Patriots* prepared to fight the most powerful navy in the world.

About 1,200 members of the South Carolina *militia* were responsible for defending Charleston. The militia was

made up of soldiers who volunteered to serve when needed, without pay. They carried their own weapons and did not have much military training. Some 435 soldiers were stationed at a fort on Sullivan's Island and ordered to guard the harbor. Colonel William Moultrie was in charge of the defenders. One of the officers serving under him was a major named Francis Marion.

No paintings were made of Francis Marion when he was alive, so all the pictures of him are based upon the writings of people who knew or met him. He was short—barely five feet tall—with a slim, awkward-looking body, a thin face, and dark eyes. Marion was quiet and serious. Although he did not look like a leader, he had a way of inspiring the men who served under him.

AN UNFINISHED FORT

Fort Sullivan was supposed to have been protected on all sides by thick stone walls. But the fort had not been completed—only the east and south walls, facing the harbor, had been finished. Also, there had not been enough stone to build the walls, so the soldiers used palmetto logs instead. Fort Sullivan had only 30 cannons, while the 50 ships of the British fleet carried 270 cannons. Major General Charles Lee, commander of the American army in the South, was so sure the British would capture the fort that he did not give the defenders very much gunpowder.

On June 28, the British warships moved into Charleston harbor and began to fire on Fort Sullivan. But their attack did not go well. Rather than destroying the fort's walls, the British cannonballs simply sank into the soft palmetto logs. And because the harbor was shallow in some places, the British ships had trouble maneuvering without running aground. British General Henry Clinton landed troops on another island, hoping they could wade through the water and attack Sullivan's Island from the rear. However, the water was too deep for the British soldiers to cross, and they had to return to their ships.

Meanwhile, the Patriots were dealing with their own problems. Because of the fort's shape, only 25 cannons could return fire. Also, the Americans had only enough powder for each cannon to fire 28 rounds, so every shot had

This drawing shows the British fleet in Charleston harbor during the attack on Fort Sullivan. To the right is the burning ship *Actaeon*. The woodcut was first published in London in August 1776.

During the Battle of Fort Sullivan, Marion commanded a battery of cannon on the left side of the unfinished fort.

to count. Marion and the other defenders aimed carefully, and soon four British warships had been damaged. One, the *Bristol,* had been hit 70 times. Three other ships became stuck on a ***shoal*** as they tried to sail around the fort and attack an unprotected side. The British had to abandon and burn one ship, the *Actaeon.* As it became clear that the fort could withstand the British attack, General Lee rushed more gunpowder and ammunition to Fort Sullivan. Finally, the enemy fleet withdrew. As the ships sailed from the harbor, Marion was granted permission to fire a parting shot.

A SURPRISING VICTORY

The Battle of Fort Sullivan was a great victory for the Patriots. Although 17 Americans had been killed, at least 115 British sailors had died and several warships had been badly damaged. The British had wasted 32,000 pounds of gunpowder firing thousands of rounds at the fort, causing little damage. The Americans needed only 5,000 pounds of powder to drive them away.

—FAST FACT—

The palmetto tree appears on the state flag of South Carolina because of its importance in protecting Fort Sullivan in 1776.

The defenders of Fort Sullivan gave hope to the Patriot cause. They had stood against the most fearsome navy in the world with cool gallantry and won a battle against dire odds. Most importantly, their successful defense of Fort Sullivan caused the British to abandon their plans to invade the southern colonies in 1776. Thanks to their improbable victory, Francis Marion and the other soldiers were celebrated as heroes throughout South Carolina. Within a few years, however, Marion would take on an even more important role as a Patriot leader during the American Revolution.

2

FROM BOY TO SOLDIER

During the 17th century, the British began to establish permanent settlements in North America. In 1670, English settlers founded the city of Charleston. It would become a major city in the Carolina colony, which was established by royal decree in 1712. In 1729, the colony was divided into North Carolina and South Carolina.

The English were not the only settlers in Carolina. In France, the government persecuted a group of people known as **Huguenots** because of their religious beliefs. Roman Catholicism was the official religion of France, but the Huguenots were Protestants who did not obey Catholic teachings. Many Huguenots left France for America, hoping

to freely practice their religion. Among the Huguenots who came to South Carolina were Judith and Benjamin Marion. Around 1685 the Marions settled in a fertile area of South Carolina called St. James Parish, located between Charleston and the Santee River. They lived near other Huguenot families.

Around 1715, the Marions' oldest son, Gabriel, married a Huguenot girl named Esther Cordes. Gabriel and Esther Marion moved up the Santee River to St. John's Parish and built a home at Goatfield Plantation. They had six children: Esther,

F. Delfinum

Huguenots land on the coast of South Carolina, circa 1562. Francis Marion was descended from Huguenots who had fled persecution in France.

Isaac, Gabriel, Benjamin, Job, and Francis, who was born in 1732. As an infant, Francis was a small, sickly child. His friend Peter Horry, who served with Francis Marion during the Revolution and later wrote a biography of him, noted that "at his birth [Marion] was not larger than a New England lobster." But Francis survived and grew stronger. When he was about five or six years old, Francis's parents moved to a new plantation in Prince George, located on Winyah Bay near Georgetown.

MARION'S CHILDHOOD

Very little is known about Francis Marion's early life. No one knows for certain whether Francis went to school in Georgetown, or for how long. It is possible that, like other boys at that time, Francis learned some reading, writing, and math at home. The letters and military reports he wrote as an adult show that he was not a very good writer. When he was old enough, Francis began to work on his uncle's plantation. He did not want to be a farmer, though. Georgetown was a port, with ships coming and going every day, and Francis dreamed of a life at sea.

When Francis was about 15, his parents agreed to let him join a ship's crew. The ship sailed to the Caribbean, but sank on the way home. The captain, Francis, and five other crewmen managed to escape in a small boat, but they had no food and only rainwater to drink. After a week adrift,

during which two of the crewmen died, the boat reached land. This cured Francis's desire for adventure at sea.

During the next few years, Francis's brothers and sister married and moved away to new homes, leaving him behind with his parents. When Francis was 18 his father died, and he found himself responsible for taking care of his mother and the family farm.

Four years after Francis's father died, a conflict that became known as the French and Indian War began. For many years France and Britain had been struggling for control of North America. France had claimed most of Canada and the land along the Mississippi River, while the British had established 13 smaller colonies along the Atlantic coast. When the fighting began, most Native American tribes sided with the French. The Indians felt the French traders treated them with respect, while the British were arrogant invaders who wanted to steal their land.

FIGHTING THE CHEROKEE

In the South, the Cherokee were among the most powerful tribes. They could call upon thousands of warriors for battle. For the first few years of the war, the Cherokee had a peace treaty with the British. However, in 1760 the Cherokee switched sides and began to attack British settlers in South Carolina. To defend the colony, the local government raised a *regiment* of militia, while the British sent

1,200 soldiers commanded by Lieutenant Colonel James Grant. Francis Marion joined the militia regiment as a first lieutenant, serving under Captain William Moultrie.

In 1761, the militia joined Grant's British troops on the hunt for Cherokee raiders. The Indians knew their hilly, thickly forested terrain well and used it to their advantage, engaging in **guerrilla warfare**. In June, near a Cherokee village called Etchoee, Lieutenant Marion was sent ahead of the army with 30 men to scout a wooded hill. As Marion's men moved forward, the Cherokee, yelling their battle cry,

SOUTH CAROLINA, 1732–1763

attacked from hiding. Soon 21 of Marion's men were dead or wounded. Despite this, Marion held his position until the rest of the army arrived to help. The battle raged for several hours, until the Cherokee retreated.

The defeat at Etchoee seemed to have broken the Cherokees' will to fight. Over 100 of the best Cherokee warriors had been killed. Over the next month, Colonel Grant's soldiers burned Etchoee and 15 other Indian villages. Finally, the Cherokee chief asked for peace.

Indian scouts guide French soldiers through the wilderness during the French and Indian War. During his service against the Cherokee, Marion observed the burning of numerous villages. His early biographer Mason Weems wrote that Marion was shocked by this destruction.

Marion's experience during the Cherokee War taught him how to use the terrain to his advantage and gave him his first taste of leadership. Marion's superiors praised his courage. "He was an active, brave and hardy soldier, and an excellent partisan officer," Moultrie later wrote about Marion's service against the Cherokee.

When the fighting ended, Marion returned to his farm. His combat service gained him a reputation as brave and dependable. Most of his neighbors liked him and considered Marion gentle and kind. He was a successful rice farmer, and in 1773 he was able to purchase a large plantation on the Santee River near Eutaw Springs, which he called Pond Bluff. Like other farmers, Marion used slaves to help run his plantation. When he was not working on the plantation, Marion enjoyed hunting and fishing. He often spent his spare time exploring the swamps, creeks, and fields near his home. For Marion, life in South Carolina was pleasant and peaceful.

—FAST FACT—

During the 18th century, slavery was a fact of life in the American colonies. Although like other rice farmers, Francis Marion owned slaves, no records have survived that indicate how he treated them. Historians do know that during the Revolution both black and white Americans fought with Marion's men in South Carolina.

RISING TENSIONS

Tensions were growing in the American colonies, though. The French and Indian War had ended in 1763 with the

British in control of North America. However, the war had been very expensive, so the British Parliament decided that Americans should pay extra taxes. In addition, to keep peace with Native Americans, in 1763 Britain's King George III had declared that Americans could not settle in lands west of the Appalachian Mountains. The restrictions and taxes made many colonists angry, but there was nothing they could do. The colonies could not elect representatives to Parliament, so they had no say in British government policies.

During the 1760s and early 1770s, colonial leaders asked King George to change his government's policies. When the king refused, some colonists decided that the only way to ensure their freedom was to break away from Britain completely. The colonists who favored independence became known as Patriots.

In South Carolina, most Patriots were wealthy planters who lived in the lowlands along the coast. They grew rice and *indigo*, crops that could be exported to Britain and other countries. One reason these planters opposed British policies was because higher taxes restricted trade and made goods from Britain more expensive. In the interior, or backcountry, more of the colonists were Loyalists who wanted to remain part of the British Empire. Most of the Loyalists owned small farms and did not import or export goods, so the British taxes did not affect them as much.

American minutemen and British soldiers clash at Lexington, Massachusetts. The battles of Lexington and Concord on April 19, 1775, are generally considered the start of the American Revolution.

THE REVOLUTION BEGINS

In April 1775, fighting between Patriots and British soldiers erupted in Massachusetts. News of the conflict quickly spread throughout the colonies, and the next month representatives from the colonies met in Philadelphia to discuss the situation. The Continental Congress, as this assembly became known, decided to create an army to defend the colonies. An experienced soldier from Virginia named George Washington was placed in command.

Soldiers in the new Continental Army were unlike militia in several ways. Militiamen were only called to serve when there was a threat to the colony. They usually served for short periods of time, then returned home to tend to their farms

or families. **Continentals** were full-time soldiers. They were paid for their service and received better weapons and more training, but had to remain with the army at all times.

As the rebellion spread, the Patriots replaced the king's royal governors with new elected legislatures. Francis Marion and his brother, Job, were both chosen as representatives to the South Carolina Provincial Congress. When this assembly met in June 1775, Francis Marion supported its decision to raise two militia regiments to defend South Carolina. Marion agreed to serve, and the 43-year-old veteran was made a captain in the Second Regiment.

3

DEFENDING SOUTH CAROLINA

One of Captain Marion's first jobs was to help quell a rebellion in the colony. After forcing the royal governor to leave South Carolina, Patriot leaders had arrested a number of prominent Loyalists. This led to a Loyalist rebellion in the backcountry, and Marion's company was sent to keep Loyalists from capturing an *armory* in Dorchester.

By December 1775 the Loyalists had been defeated. Marion and his company were next sent to Charleston, where they worked to build the city's defenses. In February 1776, Marion was promoted to major. Thanks in part to his

In this 1775 drawing published in London, an ugly crowd of armed Patriots forces a Loyalist to sign a promise not to fight. Such events did occur in South Carolina after Patriots suppressed the Loyalist revolt in December 1775.

hard work, the British were repulsed when they attacked Fort Sullivan in June 1776.

In September 1776, Marion's Second Regiment was made part of the Continental Army. Two months later, Marion was promoted to lieutenant colonel, making him the regiment's second-in-command. In September 1778, Marion took over as commander of the Second Regiment.

A RESPECTED LEADER

According to stories later written by his men, Lieutenant Colonel Marion was admired because he was a good leader who tried to take care of his troops. But he was also a demanding commander. Marion did not want his men to have long hair, and insisted that they be clean and sober. Because of Marion's discipline, his men had more confidence and pride than some other Continental units.

But things were quiet in South Carolina between 1776 and 1778, and the Second Regiment did not see much action. The Loyalists of South Carolina had promised not to fight against the colony's Patriot government, and the British army was busy fighting in the North.

A major victory for the Americans occurred in October 1777, when a Continental Army commanded by General Horatio Gates captured the British army of General John Burgoyne near Saratoga, New York. The victory helped convince France to help the Americans. French leaders saw the

revolution as a chance to hurt Britain, their greatest rival, but they had not wanted to become involved until the Americans proved they could win. In early 1778, the French signed an alliance with the Americans. France soon began sending weapons and soldiers to help the Continental Army.

A NEW STRATEGY

The French alliance forced Britain to change its strategy. For three years, General Howe had waged war primarily in the northern colonies. In May 1778, General Henry Clinton replaced Howe as the British commander in North America. Clinton had been in charge of the failed British attack on Charleston in 1776, but still believed in the plan. Clinton decided to shift the war into the South, and in the fall of 1778 he sent a British army to invade Georgia. In December, the British captured the seaport at Savannah. As Clinton had hoped, after the British arrived Loyalists in Georgia rose up and fought against the Patriots.

In September 1779, Marion led his regiment into Georgia as part of a joint French-American attempt to recapture Savannah. However, the Patriots failed and had to withdraw. By the end of 1779, all of Georgia was under British control.

Heartened by this foothold, Clinton next turned toward Charleston. Late in 1779, he sailed from New York with an army of 8,500 men. The British landed near Savannah, then marched north into South Carolina.

THE SIEGE OF CHARLESTON

In February 1780, Marion's regiment was ordered back to Charleston to help defend the city. While there, Marion was invited to a party on March 19. Once everyone arrived, the host of the party locked the doors, and many of the guests began to get drunk. Marion did not like alcohol— he preferred to drink water with a little vinegar—and was not having much fun. He looked for a way to leave the party without being seen. Finding an open second-story

American and French soldiers attack the British fortifications at Savannah, Georgia, in October 1779. Marion participated in the siege of Savannah, which failed to drive out the British.

George Washington described General Benjamin Lincoln as an "active, spirited, sensible man," but Lincoln's decision to defend Charleston in 1780 was a serious blunder that led to one of the worst American defeats of the war.

window, he jumped out. Unfortunately, he broke his ankle when he landed on the ground. The injury kept Marion from participating in the defense of Charleston, and he walked with a limp for the rest of his life.

General Benjamin Lincoln, commander of the Continental Army in the South, was an experienced veteran. George Washington had ordered Lincoln to keep his army intact, and to only engage the enemy if there was a way to escape. In Charleston, however, Lincoln was in a difficult position. Politicians in South Carolina insisted that he defend the city. Lincoln decided to stay, but he ordered all officers unfit for duty to leave town. Because Marion's ankle had not yet healed, he was among those officers who left. He stayed with relatives who lived on a plantation along the Santee River.

Soon Marion learned that the Redcoats had arrived at Charleston and cut off Lincoln's army. On May 12, 1780, Charleston surrendered, and 5,000 soldiers, including General Lincoln and most of Marion's Second Regiment,

were taken prisoner. It was one of the worst American defeats of the war.

THE BRITISH TAKE CONTROL

The Patriot government of South Carolina was forced to flee, as Clinton sent troops to capture important towns like Augusta, Camden, Ninety-Six, and Georgetown. As the Redcoats spread out across the countryside, Loyalists turned out with their muskets to help them. The Patriots were discouraged. Believing the war for independence was lost, many agreed to stop fighting. Within a few weeks, Clinton was able to report to Lord Germain, the king's trusted advisor, "there are few men in South Carolina who are not our prisoners, or in arms with us."

But Clinton made a big mistake in June 1780, when he declared that everyone in South Carolina who did not swear an oath of loyalty to the king would be considered a rebel. The Patriots who had promised to stop fighting were angry. They had expected to be *neutral*

Sir Henry Clinton permitted his soldiers and their Loyalist allies to use brutal tactics against the Patriots. This angered many Americans who might otherwise have submitted to British rule, and they soon began to fight back.

until the Revolutionary War ended, but if they took the oath they could be forced to fight on the British side. Also, there were many people in South Carolina who had not supported either the Patriots or the Loyalists. These colonists just wanted to be left alone, and did not want to fight for the British. When a backcountry leader named John James refused to take the oath, the British threatened to arrest and hang him. James escaped, and many colonists who had not previously taken sides joined the Patriots.

CIVIL WAR IN SOUTH CAROLINA

Atrocities committed by the British and their Loyalist allies added to the unrest. Because the Patriots had intimidated Loyalists during the early years of the war, when the British arrived the Loyalists saw a chance for revenge. Loyalist militias killed or arrested Patriots and looted and burned their homes and businesses. British troops also used these ruthless tactics, believing they would scare the Patriots into giving up. Their strategy backfired. Patriots began fighting back, and a savage civil war erupted in South Carolina.

The Patriots were at a disadvantage, however, as long as there was no Continental Army in South Carolina to oppose the British Army. The Continental Congress desperately wanted to regain control of the colony, and sent Horatio Gates to take charge of a new American army in the

Horatio Gates was considered one of America's best generals because of his great victory at Saratoga in 1777. Although George Washington objected, Congress chose Gates to take command of the Continental Army in the South in 1780.

South. In previous campaigns, Gates had shown a talent for building an army and preparing it to fight. But although he had commanded the victorious American army at Saratoga in October 1777, battlefield tactics were not his strength. During the Saratoga campaign Gates had stayed away from the fighting, allowing **subordinates** like Benedict Arnold and Daniel Morgan to lead the Continentals into battle.

When Gates arrived at the American camp in North Carolina in July 1780, the army was in bad shape. There were fewer than 1,500 healthy Continentals, and they were short of food, weapons, ammunition, and other supplies. Other American officers urged the newly arrived commander to spend time training and supplying his army. Gates did not listen to their advice. Instead, he started the army on the road to South Carolina to face the British.

MARION REJOINS THE ARMY

The American force gradually grew as militia from North and South Carolina joined the Continental Army. Some

Continentals who had escaped the capture of Charleston also joined the Americans. Among them was Francis Marion, still hurting from his broken ankle. He rode into the camp with a number of other men from South Carolina, including Peter Horry. Gates did not think much of Marion, and neither did the other Continentals. Colonel Otho Williams described Marion's men as "distinguished by small black leather caps and the wretchedness of their attire; their number did not exceed twenty men and boys, some white, some black, but most of them miserably equipped."

On August 15, 1780, Gates sent Marion to take charge of a militia unit that had formed in the northeastern part of South Carolina. Marion was told to raid British camps and destroy any boats he found on the Santee River. Gates hoped to surround and capture the British army, just as he had trapped Burgoyne's army at Saratoga. If Gates defeated the Redcoats at Camden, Marion's actions would prevent the British from escaping across the river.

Marion, accompanied by Horry, an African-American slave named Oscar, and the rest of his followers, arrived at Williamsburg and assumed command of about 500 men. He organized

—FAST FACT—

A young soldier named William James wrote about meeting Francis Marion at General Gates's camp: "He was dressed in a close round-bodied crimson jacket, of a coarse texture, and wore a leather cap, part of the uniform of the second regiment, with a silver crescent in front, inscribed with the words, 'Liberty or death.'"

the militia into companies, and sent the men to carry out Gates's orders. But while they were burning boats, Marion received terrible news. When the American army arrived at Camden, Gates had made a serious tactical mistake and the British had destroyed his army.

Most Continental officers knew that poorly trained militia units were not reliable in battle. The inexperienced part-time soldiers often ran away when British troops charged with their bayonets. But at Camden on August 16, 1780, Gates had placed his militia in a key spot on his battle line. When the British charged, the militia broke and ran, and the British surrounded and captured most of his Continental soldiers. Gates himself had run away from the battle, followed by the remnants of his shattered army.

Two days later, a crack British unit caught and destroyed a regiment of South Carolina militia commanded by Thomas Sumter at Fishing Creek. Now, the only American force left to oppose the British in South Carolina was Francis Marion's small militia unit.

4

THE SWAMP FOX

Unlike General Gates, Marion understood that his militia would not be able to stand up to British troops in an open battle. He realized that his men would be most effective if they used surprise and deception to disrupt the enemy's plans. They would use horses to move quickly, attacking small British detachments and isolated supply wagons when they saw an opportunity. They would avoid capture or battle when outnumbered by hiding in nearby swamps and creeks.

Marion soon had an opportunity to practice his guerrilla tactics. His spies reported that 150 American prisoners being taken from Camden to Charleston were spending the night at a nearby plantation. The colonel quickly hatched a

plan to free the Americans. On August 25, 1780, Marion and his militia raided the plantation, surprising the British guards. They killed or captured 22 Redcoats and freed the prisoners. But to Marion's surprise, only a few of the American soldiers joined him. Most thought the war was hopeless, and wanted to go home and stop fighting.

British General Charles Cornwallis was annoyed when he learned about Marion's daring raid. Cornwallis was an experienced and respected leader who had taken charge of the British army in South Carolina when Clinton returned to New York in June. Under his leadership the Americans had been crushed at the Battle of Camden. He sent British troops, as well as Loyalist militias, to find Marion and stop him from raiding the British.

General Charles Cornwallis's plan to invade North Carolina was frustrated by Marion's hit-and-run tactics. The British general knew that he could not allow an enemy army to operate behind his lines, so he sent soldiers to catch Marion.

Marion's men used horses to strike suddenly, then escape into the woods and swamps. According to reports written by men who served under Marion, the general wore a black cap like the one in this illustration. On the front of Marion's cap was a silver crescent engraved with the word "Liberty."

This would prove to be difficult. Marion and his men were very familiar with the swampy terrain. Before the main British force could respond, Marion's brigade would disappear. Horses were important for this type of warfare, for they allowed the Patriots to hit their enemies quickly and then run away. Marion knew that if his men did not have horses, they could not raid the British and escape.

DEALING WITH MANY HARDSHIPS

Marion had a constant problem keeping his militia together. His men were volunteers who could not serve for long periods of time. They had to go home and take care of their farms, especially at planting time. As a result, Marion's militia often fluctuated in strength, sometimes dropping to as few as 20 or 30 men.

The most important problem for Marion, though, was avoiding capture. A force of about 250 Loyalists, led by Major Micajah Ganey, posed a great danger when they began moving down the Pee Dee River in early September 1780. The Loyalists knew the area well, but Marion's men stayed alert. One morning a squadron commanded by Peter Horry surprised Ganey and 45 soldiers who were looking for Marion's camp. When the Patriots charged, the Loyalists ran away.

The rest of Ganey's men were three miles away, so Marion moved with about 50 men to attack. The Tories had

greater numbers, so Marion allowed the enemy to see him and then retreated into the brush and trees of an area called Blue Savannah. As the Loyalists followed them, the rebels attacked from ambush. Four of Marion's men were wounded, but the Tories again turned and ran. The ferocious attack by Marion and his men scared the Loyalists. Most returned to their farms and refused to fight any more. The victory encouraged local Patriots, though, and 60 more men joined Marion.

ESCAPE TO THE SWAMPS

But Ganey was not the only Loyalist trying to find Marion's men. Another militia, commanded by Major James Wemyss, joined up with a unit of British soldiers. The combined force of 800 men set out for a fort Marion had built near the Pee Dee River. Marion knew his few hundred militiamen were not strong enough to oppose Wemyss. He told most of his men to return to their homes. To escape Wemyss, Marion and about 60 men rode into North Carolina and hid in the Great White Marsh of what is today Columbus County.

Life in the swamp was tough. Marion's men had little food, no tents, and few blankets. In the Great White Marsh, the water was of poor quality, and it bred mosquitoes. Some men became ill from drinking the foul water. Others got malaria spread by the mosquitoes and had to go home. Marion's Brigade ate what they could find, including sweet

potatoes, fish, and pork from wild hogs. In most armies, officers lived better than their soldiers, but this was not the case with Marion. The 48-year-old general shared the hardships of his younger men.

Without Marion's militia to stop the Loyalists, Wemyss and his men burned churches and farms, stole horses, and killed people suspected of helping the Patriots. He became one of the most hated men in the South. By September 20, 1780, Wemyss reported to Cornwallis that he had "burnt and laid waste about 50 houses and Plantations, mostly

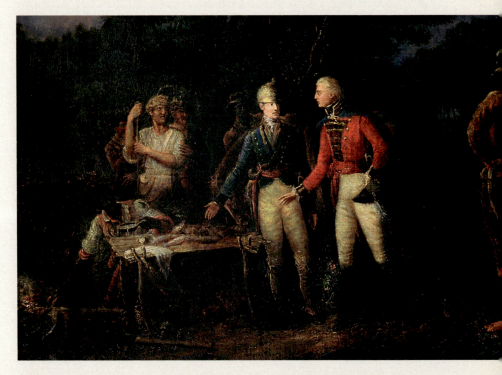

Although food and supplies were scarce in the Carolina swamps, Marion managed to sustain his men's morale. In this painting, Marion invites a captured British officer to share a meager meal of sweet potatoes at their grubby camp. Behind them are Marion's ragged soldiers.

belonging to People who have either broke their **Paroles** or Oaths of Allegiance, and are now in Arms against us."

When word of these atrocities reached Marion and his men, they decided they had to strike back. They got on their horses and rode for South Carolina, passing through a swamp and crossing the Little Pee Dee River. As they traveled, angry colonists volunteered to join Marion, increasing his numbers.

VICTORIOUS RAIDS

On September 28, 1780, Marion's men learned that 46 Loyalist soldiers, led by Colonel John Ball, were camped about 20 miles northeast of Georgetown at a place called Shepherd's Ferry on Black Mingo Creek. Marion's men silently surrounded the enemy, then attacked in the middle of the night. The fighting was over quickly. Three of Ball's men were killed and 13 were wounded; the rest were taken prisoner. Two of Marion's men were killed. The Americans captured ammunition, guns, and several horses. Francis claimed the colonel's horse, renaming it "Ball" in memory of his victory. This raid and other midnight attacks scared Loyalists in South Carolina. Every success brought Marion new recruits.

Marion was not the only American leader fighting guerrilla war. Men like Thomas Sumter and Andrew Pickens also led Patriot groups that fought back against the Loyalists. Unfortunately, the civil war in South Carolina was very bitter,

Marion's men use flat-bottomed rafts on one of their many crossings of the Pee Dee River. Marion is the mounted officer on the left, with the cloak around his shoulders.

and soldiers on both sides committed horrible atrocities. Sumter allowed his men to **plunder** and burn the homes of Loyalists in revenge for the burning of Patriot homes.

Like Sumter, Marion wanted to keep Loyalists from fighting, but he did not let his men terrorize civilians. He believed mistreating Loyalists would make them more likely to resist the Patriots. Men who served with him said that Marion only attacked military targets. "Of all the men who ever drew a sword, Marion was one of the most humane," Peter Horry later wrote. "He not only prevented cruelty in his own presence, but strictly forbade it in his absence." His men sometimes took food, supplies, horses, or weapons they

needed from Loyalist farmers, but they always gave *receipts*. These promised that if the Patriots won the war, the new government would repay Loyalists for their goods.

CORNWALLIS IS CHECKED

The success of Marion's militia angered Cornwallis. He wanted to invade and conquer North Carolina, but needed the rebels in South Carolina to stop fighting. Although Cornwallis moved part of his army north, he was afraid Marion would attack the British forts in South Carolina. The loss of a fort meant a break in the army's supply chain, and would reduce British control over that area of the colony.

On October 7, 1780, Cornwallis's plan suffered a major setback when Patriots defeated Major Patrick Ferguson at the Battle of King's Mountain. Cornwallis needed Ferguson's Loyalist militia to protect his army's supply line. Without it, he had to break off the invasion of North Carolina. Cornwallis returned to South Carolina, and focused on stopping Marion and other Patriots from stirring up rebellion.

Marion's men continued their successful attacks. On October 25, Marion and 152 men attacked 200 Loyalists commanded by Colonel Samuel Tynes at Tearcoat Swamp. The Patriots attacked at midnight and surprised the Loyalists. They killed six men and captured 23. The rest of Tynes's militia ran away, leaving their muskets and horses for the

Patriots. Some of the captured Loyalists even switched sides and joined Marion's men.

THE HUNT FOR MARION'S MEN

With the South Carolina countryside rising against the British, Cornwallis sent his best troops after Marion. The British Legion, a mixed force of cavalry and infantry, had won many battles against the Americans. The Patriots hated and feared Lieutenant Colonel Banastre Tarleton, the Legion's commander. Tarleton was a handsome, intelligent officer who was willing to do whatever was necessary to end the rebellion, even if that meant killing rebels and burning their homes. One event shortly after the capture of Charleston made Tarleton infamous. In May 1780, at a place called the Waxhaws, the British Legion had killed hundreds of unarmed Continental who were trying to surrender. Because of this brutal massacre, Tarleton's enemies called him "Bloody Ban" or "Ban the Butcher."

Tarleton and the British Legion set out to find Marion in early November 1780. They questioned colonists to find out where Marion's Brigade was hiding. The cunning British leader developed a plan to draw Marion into an ambush. Tarleton had his men light campfires, then hide in the woods nearby. He hoped that Marion and his men would attack their deserted camp, so the British could surprise them.

This painting shows Banastre Tarleton, wearing the green jacket of the British Legion, reaching for his sword. Tarleton was a ruthless commander, and his Legion was the most feared British unit operating in South Carolina.

The plan almost worked. Marion's men were cautiously heading toward the British camp on November 7, 1780, when they were warned that Tarleton was waiting for them. Marion decided to withdraw. When Tarleton learned the next day that his plan had been foiled, he sent his horsemen after Marion. They chased the Americans for 26 miles, until Marion and his men reached Ox Swamp, about 20 miles from the town of Kingstree.

Tarleton's men were tired from the long, hard ride, and he was not willing to pursue the Americans into the swamp. "Come, my boys! Let us go back and we will find the Gamecock [Thomas Sumter]," he shouted, according to a later account. "But as for this dammed old fox, the devil himself could not catch him."

As Tarleton left Ox Swamp, he burned 30 houses belonging to Patriots. This destroyed any sympathy that locals might have had for the British. The Americans enjoyed hearing stories about Marion's hit-and-run victories, and of how he had escaped Tarleton's British Legion. They soon gave the wily and determined Patriot a new nickname—the Swamp Fox.

5

TURNING TIDE IN THE SOUTH

When Tarleton returned to the British camp, he reported that Marion's militia had been routed. "The Country seems now convinced of the error of Insurrection," he wrote to Cornwallis. "I have used my best Abilities to settle the Affairs of this part of the Province . . . the total Destruction of Mr. Marion had been accomplished." Cornwallis was pleased—the way Tarleton told the story, the Swamp Fox would no longer be a problem.

Marion had not been defeated, though. He led his men to a new hiding place on Snow Island, and prepared to continue the fight against the British. Snow Island was an excellent place to hide, because it was protected on all sides by water. To the east was the Pee Dee River. To the north was

Snow Island was Marion's favorite hiding place. Deep in a wild area of swamps and rivers, surrounded by cypress trees and canebrakes, it was difficult to find.

Lynches Creek, to the south and west was Clark's Creek, and on the west was Snow Lake. On the island itself was a house and barn surrounded by a thick forest. Marion and his men built shelters for themselves, and bins to store their food. Marion's slave Oscar stayed at Snow Island to watch the camp while the men were raiding.

SADNESS AND FRUSTRATION

Marion's men desperately needed ammunition, salt, clothes, and other supplies. In mid-November, the colonel devised a plan to capture Georgetown, where all the goods his militia needed were stored. However, when Marion's 400 men tried to sneak up on the village, British soldiers spotted them and spoiled their attack. Marion's nephew, Gabriel Marion, was captured by a group of Loyalists. When they learned who Gabriel was, they murdered him. Marion mourned for his nephew, the first member of his family who had been killed.

Despite his personal sorrow, Marion kept up his attacks. He sent patrols throughout the Williamsburg countryside to encourage the Patriots and frighten the Loyalists. His militia was still not strong enough to do more than just harass the British, though. He needed the support of the Continental Army, as well as food, ammunition, and salt. On November 20, he wrote to Horatio Gates, asking when the Continental Army would return to South Carolina. "Many

of my people has left me & gone over to the Enemy, for they think that we have no Army coming in." Two days later, he wrote another letter to Gates: "The People here is not to be depended on for I seldom have the same set [of militiamen] a fortnight [two weeks], & until the Grand Army is on the Banks of Santee, it will be the same." Gates, who was in North Carolina trying to rebuild the shattered Continental Army, never answered the general's letters.

Marion's attacks were so effective that by the end of November, the Patriots controlled the Williamsburg area. But this success brought a new problem. Many of his volunteers wanted to return to their families. The British had burned their homes, and they wanted to rebuild now that the region was under Patriot control. Marion had no choice but to let the men go home until he needed them again.

GOOD NEWS FOR MARION

December 1780 brought better news. Marion was pleased to learn that he had been promoted to brigadier general. More good news soon followed. Nathanael Greene, one of the most capable American generals, had been appointed to replace Gates. Greene faced a tough challenge, though. He had only about 1,500 trained soldiers, while the British had over 8,000 men in South Carolina alone. To succeed, Greene knew that he had to pick at the British wherever they were weak, until he could increase his own strength. The Redcoats were spread

Nathanael Greene was one of George Washington's most trusted generals, and the only man the commander-in-chief believed could salvage the desperate situation in the South. Greene immediately recognized the value of Marion's militia, and ordered them to continue harassing the British while he prepared an army to fight.

out at different forts throughout South Carolina. Small units like the one Francis Marion led could get information about enemy troop movements, destroy British supplies, and maybe even capture some forts.

Greene ordered Marion to spy on and **harass** the British. "Your services in the lower part of South Carolina, in awing the Tories and preventing the enemy from extending their limits, have been very important," Greene wrote to Marion. "And it is my earnest desire that you continue where you are until further advice from me. . . . I like your plan of frequently shifting your ground. It frequently prevents a surprise and perhaps a total loss of your party. Until a more permanent army can be collected than is in the field at present, we must endeavor to keep up a partisan war, and preserve the tide of sentiment among the people in our favor as much as possible."

Marion was thrilled at finally being put to good tactical use. He called out the militia again, organizing the unit

that became known as Marion's Brigade, and began to raid British and Loyalist outposts around Georgetown. In one clash, Marion's men encountered the Loyalist Major Ganey and his reformed militia. Once again, they dispersed Ganey's men. In another raid, Marion's men captured 150 tons of salt, a valuable commodity that was in short supply in war-torn South Carolina. Salt was needed to preserve meat and add flavor to food. Marion's men used some of the salt, but he ordered that the rest be given to Patriot families in the Williamsburg district. This made the general even more popular.

The activities of Marion's Brigade were more important than the Swamp Fox might have realized. In January 1781, a force of Continentals and militia led by General Daniel Morgan defeated the British Legion at the Battle of Cowpens. This important victory might not have been possible were it not for General Marion. The British, worried about Marion's Brigade, had been forced to keep some soldiers back to protect their supplies in South Carolina. This meant Tarleton could not get reinforcements before his battle with Morgan.

LEE ARRIVES TO HELP

To help Marion harass the British, General Greene sent Lieutenant Colonel Henry "Light Horse Harry" Lee with a detachment of Continental *dragoons*. Lee's men were skilled

horsemen and well-trained fighters. Like Marion, Lee was a demanding leader who was loved by his men. In fact, Marion's friend Peter Horry called Lee "a second Marion."

The two commanders made plans to attack Georgetown. The assault began before dawn on January 24. The Americans captured some Loyalist officers, but the British troops refused to come out of their fort to fight the Americans. The Americans could not get in to fight because they had no cannons to knock down the walls. Knowing that when the sun rose his men would be easy targets for British sharpshooters, Marion ordered his men to withdraw. Soon after this, Lee and his men marched north to rejoin Greene's army.

Marion was sorry to see Lee go, but he soon had other problems. Cornwallis had again taken part of his army into North Carolina, leaving Lord Francis Rawdon in charge of British troops in South Carolina. Rawdon decided to eliminate Marion's Brigade by attacking from two directions. He ordered Colonel John Watson and a mixed

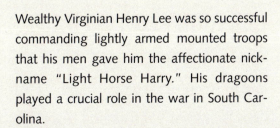

Wealthy Virginian Henry Lee was so successful commanding lightly armed mounted troops that his men gave him the affectionate nickname "Light Horse Harry." His dragoons played a crucial role in the war in South Carolina.

force of British troops and Loyalists to march down the Santee River and attack Marion. At the same time, a group of Loyalists from New York commanded by Colonel Welbore Doyle would march down the Pee Dee River and cut off Marion's retreat.

FIGHTING OFF THE BRITISH

On March 6, 1781, Marion's and Watson's men clashed in an open field near Wiboo Swamp. Marion's men fought bravely, but the American militia was no match for the British regulars, and they were forced to retreat. Over the next few days, the British cautiously followed Marion's men as they retreated toward Georgetown. A fierce fight broke out over a key bridge across the Black River. This time, the Americans forced the British to withdraw. Watson and his men stayed in the field for several weeks, but they could not catch the Swamp Fox. Eventually, Watson decided to leave the area. Marion's Brigade ambushed the retreating British troops at the Sampit River, and 20 British soldiers were killed before Watson and his men could escape.

Like other British commanders, Watson had been frustrated by Marion's elusive tactics and midnight raids. "They will not sleep and fight like gentlemen, but like savages are eternally firing and whooping around us by night, and by day waylaying and popping at us from behind every tree," Watson wrote to Rawdon.

THE LOSS OF SNOW ISLAND

But while Marion was focused on Watson's troops, he did not realize that Doyle was looking for his base on Snow Island. Before Marion could get back to the hideout, Doyle arrived and destroyed the ammunition and supplies stored there, then left the area. When Marion arrived, he sent his men to chase Doyle, but the loss of the supplies on Snow Island was a devastating blow to the general.

To make matters worse, many of Marion's men wanted to go home and tend to their farms for the spring planting season. By the time Marion found a new camp at Indiantown, located east of Kingstree, he had only 70 men under his command.

Having lost most of his supplies, ammunition, and men, Marion was discouraged. He knew that both Doyle and Watson would be coming back after him. Yet he did not give up. In April, when Watson's British troops returned to the Williamsburg area, some 500 Patriot militiamen responded to Marion's call for help. Then came an unexpected surprise—Colonel Lee returned with his dragoons on April 14. Many Loyalists left Watson's camp when they learned that Continental troops had arrived, and Watson was forced to retreat again.

Lee brought exciting news. On March 15, 1781, Greene and Cornwallis had battled at a place called Guilford Courthouse in North Carolina. After a day of brutal fighting, the

Americans had pulled back. However, the battle marked a turning point in the war. The British had lost many more soldiers than the Americans, and Cornwallis decided to retreat to Wilmington, on the coast of North Carolina. The British outposts in South Carolina were isolated, and Greene had sent Lee to join Marion, hoping they could pick off the forts one by one.

ATTACK ON FORT WATSON

Marion and Lee decided to attack one of these garrisons, Fort Watson, which was located in what is today Clarendon County, South Carolina. If the Americans could capture the fort, they would get much-needed supplies and ammunition. The problem was that the fort was well defended. It was on top of an Indian mound and surrounded by trees. The British troops inside had lots of ammunition, food, and water. And Marion and Lee had no cannons to use to destroy the walls around the fort.

Realizing they could not take the fort quickly, the Americans placed it under siege on April 16, 1781. Things did not look good. The British were safe and well fed. Worse, many of Marion's men came down with *smallpox*. Some sick members of the brigade left for home. But despite the spreading illness, Marion could not allow his army to dwindle further. He declared that anyone else who left would be treated as "an Enemy to the United States."

The fort held fast until one of Marion's officers, Major Hezekiah Maham, came up with an idea: why not build a tower so they could shoot down into the fort? Marion and Lee approved, and men were sent to cut down nearby trees. On April 23, a 40-foot-tall log structure was complete and the Americans began firing into Fort Watson. The British quickly surrendered. The "Maham tower" had worked, and for the first time since the invasion of South Carolina, the Americans had captured a British fort.

MAJOR BATTLES IN THE SOUTH

When General Greene heard this good news, he took the time to pen a long letter praising Marion. "When I consider how much you have done and suffered, and under what disadvantage you have maintained your ground, I am at a loss which to admire most, your courage and fortitude, or your address and management," Greene wrote. "No man has a better claim to the public thanks, or is more generally admired than you are. History affords no instance wherein an officer has kept possession of a country under so many disadvantages as you have."

CAPTURE OF FORT MOTTE

Marion and Lee decided their next target would be Fort Motte, near the Congaree and Wateree rivers. Fort Motte was defended by about 140 British soldiers, and was not going to fall easily. The fort was actually a large plantation house that the British had fortified by digging a trench and building **earthworks**.

Lee and Marion arrived at the fort on May 8, 1781. They knew that Rawdon's troops, retreating from Greene's army after the Battle of Hobkirk's Hill, were also moving toward the fort. If the Americans could not capture the fort before Rawdon arrived, they would have to give up the siege. Marion was anxious, and frustrated with his men. Many had left for home, and the ones who remained were poorly trained and disciplined compared to Lee's Continentals.

On the night of May 11, the Americans could see Rawdon's campfires burning in the distance. Marion knew the reinforcements were just two days away, so he decided on a new tactic to end the siege. The owner of the mansion, Rebecca Motte, had been expelled from her house because she had supported the Patriots. She was living in a nearby log cabin. When Marion asked for her permission to shoot flaming arrows onto the wooden roof of the mansion to burn it down, Mrs. Motte agreed. According to Peter Horry, she even gave Marion's men a bow and arrows to use.

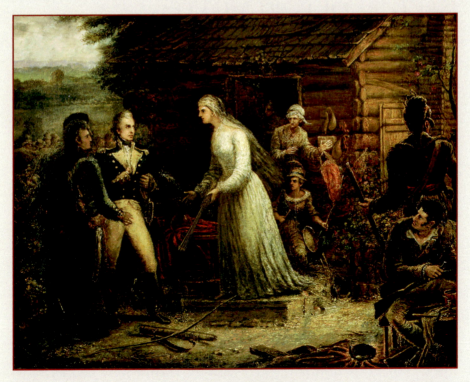

In this painting, which depicts a story told by both Peter Horry and Henry Lee, Rebecca Motte offers Marion and Lee a bow and arrows to use in burning down her house.

At noon on May 12, Lee gave the order to shoot the arrows. Soon, the roof of the house was on fire. With the flames spreading and only a few feet between the outer wall of the house and the trench, there was no place for the British to hide. They surrendered.

After the fort was captured, Mrs. Motte invited officers from both sides to dinner at her log cabin. They were impressed by her hospitality, and her kindness set them all at such ease that they dined like friends. The pleasant dinner was interrupted, though, when a message came that some of the Continental soldiers were hanging local Tories. At the news, Marion leapt from the table, grabbed his sword, and hurried to camp. He found two dead Tories under a tree, and three dragoons in the process of hanging a third man. Marion ordered the men to set the Loyalist free. As long as he was in charge of the brigade, he would not tolerate brutality.

6

THE FIGHTING ENDS

After the capture of Fort Motte, Lee's dragoons were sent to attack another British fort, while Marion's Brigade was ordered to watch Lord Rawdon's small army. While his spies watched Rawdon's progress, Marion sent most of his men to assault Georgetown again on May 29, 1781. This time, the British defenders were afraid to face Marion's Brigade. They left the village before Marion's men arrived.

Greene and the Continental Army, meanwhile, were besieging the British fort at Ninety-Six. After Marion reported that Rawdon was moving west to lift the siege, Greene ordered the South Carolina militia units to join him at Ninety-Six. Marion tried to call out the militia, but

his men were not willing to travel so far from their homes. Marion himself was reluctant to go, because he would have to serve under General Sumter, who was officially in charge of all South Carolina militia. With the few men who turned out for his call to arms, Marion moved slowly toward Ninety-Six. Before he could arrive, Greene broke off the siege. He was annoyed with the militia. Marion was not the only commander who had not responded—neither Sumter nor General Andrew Pickens had brought their men to help the Continental Army.

Sumter was a brave and aggressive commander with a mixed record in battle. He preferred to operate alone, rather than working with the Continental Army. Several times he ordered Marion's Brigade to join his own militia force, but Marion always found good reasons not to leave the Williamsburg district.

In July Marion learned that British reinforcements had landed at Charleston and were marching to join Lord Rawdon's army.

General Thomas Sumter was more aggressive than Marion, though his record in battle was not as good. Many people believed Sumter cared more for personal glory than for his men. Henry Lee later wrote about Sumter, "Enchanted with the splendor of victory, he would wade in torrents of blood to attain it."

He tried to block them, but was unable to prevent the fresh troops from reinforcing Rawdon at Orangeburg. Marion's men joined Greene's Continentals at nearby Ancrum's Plantation, on the Congaree River. When Sumter's men arrived at the American camp, Greene ordered the two generals to work together and attack British outposts between Orangeburg and Charleston.

DISASTER AT QUINBY CREEK

On July 17, the combined militia force, joined by Lee's dragoons, found that a British regiment had built fortifications at Quinby Creek. Marion and Lee felt it would be impossible to dislodge the British, but Sumter recklessly insisted on attacking. The frontal assault was a disaster. Many Americans were killed or wounded, including some 50 members of Marion's Brigade. Marion was appalled at the slaughter, and he vowed never to serve with Sumter again.

After Marion's Brigade left the area, Sumter's militia began plundering the homes of Loyalists. In response, the British attacked Georgetown and burned more than 40 homes, stores, and warehouses belonging to Patriots. But now that much of South Carolina was back in Patriot hands, leaders like Governor John Rutledge wanted to end the civil war among the colonists. Hoping to ease tensions among Patriot and Loyalist neighbors, Rutledge made plundering illegal. Sumter, offended by the order and

exhausted from campaigning, decided to give up command of his militia.

With Sumter's retirement, Marion became the senior militia leader in South Carolina. Rutledge soon gave Marion new duties. The general was told to establish martial law in the northeastern part of the colony. Marion would be responsible for raising taxes to support the war effort and establishing law and order.

CLASH AT EUTAW SPRINGS

On September 4, 1781, Marion received new orders from Greene. Cornwallis had invaded Virginia, and a Continental Army under George Washington was working with the French to trap the British commander. Washington wanted Greene to prevent the British in South Carolina from reinforcing Cornwallis. Greene ordered Marion's 400 men to join him at the American camp near Eutaw Springs. When they arrived, Greene explained his plan to attack 2,000 British troops commanded by Lieutenant Colonel Alexander Stewart. He placed Marion in charge of all the American militia, which made up more than half his army of 2,400 men.

Early in the morning, the Americans advanced on the British camp. Stewart had been warned that Greene was on the way, and he hurried to assemble battle lines. Fighting was fierce, and both sides came close to breaking. The British fell back from American bayonet charges, but British

British soldiers retreat in the face of an American charge during the Battle of Eutaw Springs. During the battle, Marion's militia showed their training by standing up to repeated British attacks. "My Brigade behaved well," the satisfied general later wrote to Peter Horry.

volleys and artillery fire took a serious toll. Casualities were high: 408 Americans and 693 British soldiers were killed or wounded. Although the British eventually forced the Americans from the battlefield and claimed victory, Stewart's army had been shattered. He was forced to retreat back toward Charleston, the only part of South Carolina still occupied by the British.

Marion's Brigade fought well. Generally, in an open battle like the one at Eutaw Springs, militia were only expected to fire two or three volleys before running away. At Eutaw Springs, Marion's men fired all their ammunition—17 rounds—before pulling back. Their conduct was a credit to Marion's leadership. "Our officers behaved with the greatest

bravery, and the militia gained much honor by their firmness," Greene later wrote.

MARION'S NEW DUTIES

After the Battle of Eutaw Springs, Marion settled into more administrative duties. He had been told to let Loyalists return to their homes in peace if they signed a promise of allegiance to the new colonial government. Marion accepted these pledges, while also taking care of his militia.

On November 9, Light Horse Harry Lee rode into Marion's camp with exciting news. Cornwallis's army had been trapped at Yorktown, Virginia, and the British general had surrendered! Lee also brought a dispatch from the Continental Congress that thanked Marion "for his wise, gallant, and decided conduct, in defending the liberties of his country."

When Governor Rutledge ordered an election for a new state assembly in December 1781, Marion was chosen as a senator representing St. John's Parish. Before the assembly met at Jacksonboro in January 1782, Marion turned command of his brigade over to Colonel Horry.

Although Marion was involved in the passage of important new laws, he found the legislature boring. When some British troops moved out of Charleston to attack his Brigade, Marion left the assembly and rejoined his men. In early June 1782, Marion's Brigade put down a Loyalist uprising headed by an old adversary, Major Ganey. About 500 Loyalists put

down their weapons and swore allegiance to the new government. Marion's last battle occurred on August 29, 1782,
when 100 British dragoons led by Major Thomas Fraser
attacked his camp. Marion's men killed four Redcoats, but
had to retreat when they ran out of ammunition.

Over the next few months, the fighting in South Carolina ended. The British left Charleston on December 14,
1782, and Greene invited Marion to a celebration of the
American victory. Never much for parties, the Swamp Fox
declined. Instead, he disbanded his militia and returned to

The British army surrenders at Yorktown, October 19, 1781. Marion and the
Patriots of South Carolina had played an important role in Cornwallis's defeat.

his plantation. Marion's house had been burned, his belongings had been destroyed or stolen, his farm animals had been eaten, and his slaves had run away. The general borrowed money and began to rebuild.

PEACETIME LEADER

Although he was no longer an active general, Marion had new duties. As a state senator, he was involved in passing laws for South Carolina. He held true to his belief that the Loyalists should be treated fairly. Marion made sure that the new government paid Loyalists for the supplies his men had taken during the war. He voted against a law that would protect Patriots who had plundered civilians. When a former Tory asked for a *pardon*, Marion spoke in his favor. "It is peace now," he told the assembly. "God has given us the victory; let us show our gratitude to heaven, which we shall not do by cruelty to man."

While not all the senators agreed with Marion, they all appreciated his wartime service. In February 1783, the South Carolina senate officially thanked him for his efforts during the revolution. And in 1784, Marion was made commander of Fort Johnson. Marion was probably given the job because he was short on money. The post came with a small salary, and was a way the grateful state could help its hero.

Although Marion appreciated the support, he was lonely. Fighting in the Revolution had left little time for a social

life, and he had never married. He began courting a childhood sweetheart, his cousin Mary Esther Videau. They liked many of the same things, and enjoyed each other's company. They married on April 20, 1786. Soon afterward, the 54-year-old general resigned from his position at Fort Johnson, and the Marions went to live at Pond Bluff. They never had any children.

Marion continued to work in the state senate. He was reelected several times, and in 1790 he helped write a new South Carolina state constitution. He also continued serving as a militia commander. When he had spare time, he and Mary would travel through the state, stopping at the sites of battles and visiting old friends.

In 1794, Marion retired from public life. Over the next year, his health grew worse and he often complained of headaches. One night, the general went to bed feeling very ill. Mary was by his side, and he told her to be strong. "I am not afraid to die," he said. On February 27, 1795, 63-year-old Francis Marion passed away. He was buried at Belle Isle on his brother Gabriel's plantation. His gravestone proclaimed that he was a man "who lived without fear, and died without reproach."

The story of Francis Marion shows how the bravery and determination of one good leader can change history. Francis Marion did not fight as long in the Revolution as some other Patriot leaders. He saw most of his combat between

Henry Lee wrote about Francis Marion: "The procurement of subsistence for his men, and the continuance of annoyance for his enemy, engrossed his entire mind. He was virtuous all over. . . . Beloved by his friends, and respected by his enemies."

SOUTH   CAROLINA
FRANCIS MARION'S GRAVE
Francis Marion died Feb. 27, 1795, in his 63rd year, and was buried here at Belle Isle Plantation, home of his brother, Gabriel. His own plantation, Pond Bluff, was about 15 miles up river and is now under Lake Marion. He was born in South Carolina, the descendant of French Huguenot emigrants. The exact date and place of his birth are unknown.

1780 and 1782. Still, this short, barely literate man proved to be an excellent guerrilla commander. Despite shortages of supplies and ammunition, his ragged volunteers kept British troops and their Loyalist allies in a constant state of fear. Marion's ability to harass and confound the British kept Patriot hopes in the South alive, and helped save the American Revolution.

Chronology

1732: Francis Marion is born in St. John's Parish, South Carolina.

1747: Francis's ship sinks in the Caribbean Sea. He returns to work on his family's farm.

1754: The first shots in what would become the French and Indian War are fired at Fort Necessity in the Ohio River Valley.

1761: In January, Francis Marion is appointed a militia lieutenant; in June, takes part in battle against the Cherokee.

1764: Britain passes the Sugar Act.

1765: Britain passes the Stamp Act.

1767: Britain passes the Townshend Acts.

1773: Marion buys a plantation, which he calls Pond Bluff, on the Santee River.

1775: In April, Patriots fight British troops at Lexington and Concord; in June, the South Carolina Provincial Congress raises two regiments of militia to defend the state from the British. Marion is made a captain in the Second Regiment; Loyalists in South Carolina rebel against the Patriot government

1776: After helping to put down the Loyalist rebellion, Marion gets promoted to major. In June, Marion takes part in the Battle of Fort Sullivan. A month later, the Declaration of Independence is written. In November, Marion is promoted to lieutenant colonel.

1777: At the Battle of Saratoga in October, Continentals and militia capture a large British army. This victory encourages France to enter the war on the American side. British commander Henry Clinton decides to shift the war to the southern colonies.

1778: In December, the British capture Savannah, Georgia.

1780: In March, in an attempt to leave a party, Marion jumps out a window and breaks his ankle. In April, on the orders of General Benjamin Lincoln, Marion leaves Charleston. In August, he assumes command of soldiers from Williamsburg. That same month, Marion frees American

prisoners being held by the British. In September, he defeats Tory forces led by Major Micjah Ganey and by Colonel John Coming Ball. In November, British Colonel Banastre Tarleton chases Marion into a swamp; afterward, Marion becomes known as the "Swamp Fox." In December, Francis is promoted to rank of brigadier general.

1781: In January, Marion's nephew, Gabriel, is killed by British troops. Around March, British Colonel Doyle destroys the hideout at Snow Island. The next month, Marion and Lieutenant Colonel Henry Lee capture Fort Watson. In May, Francis and Lee take Fort Motte. A month later, they capture Georgetown. In August, Marion becomes the senior commander of militia in South Carolina. Marion's Brigade fights at Battle of Eutaw Springs in September. On October 19, Lord Cornwallis and the British army surrender at Yorktown.

1782: Francis is elected to the South Carolina assembly in January. In August, he fights his last battle. In December, the last British soldier leaves Charleston.

1783: The South Carolina senate passes a resolution thanking Francis for his work during the Revolution.

1784: Francis Marion is appointed commandant of Fort Johnson.

1786: Francis marries his cousin, Mary Videau, in April. Around the same time, he resigns his post as commander of Fort Johnson.

1790: Francis helps write the new South Carolina state constitution.

1794: The Swamp Fox retires from the militia.

1795: Francis Marion dies on February 27.

Glossary

armory—a building in which weapons are stored.

atrocities—extremely cruel or shocking acts of violence against an enemy during wartime.

Continentals—a soldier in the American army during the Revolution. Unlike militia, Continentals served full-time and were paid for their services. They were also better trained and equipped than militia.

dragoon—a soldier who traveled on horseback but usually fought on foot. Dragoons were often armed with swords as well as short muskets called carbines.

earthworks—fortification made from soil.

guerrilla warfare—a type of fighting in which small groups of soldiers use surprise attacks against enemy troops.

harass—to annoy; to tire out an enemy by constantly attacking him.

Huguenot—French Protestants who moved to America during the 17th century to escape persecution in France.

indigo—a type of plant used to make a blue dye that could be used on clothes and paper.

Loyalist—a colonist who was loyal to Great Britain during the Revolution; also called a Tory.

militia—an army of civilian volunteers called up in emergencies to perform military service. In Colonial America, all able-bodied men were expected to serve in their colony's militia. They served without pay, and were expected to provide their own muskets.

neutral—not belonging to or supporting either side in a conflict or dispute.

pardon—to free someone from being punished for a crime.

parole—from the French parole d'honneur ("word of honor"), this was a promise made by a person taken prisoner in a battle that he would not fight again until officially exchanged for another prisoner.

Glossary

Patriot—a colonist who wanted independence from Great Britain during the Revolution; also called a Whig.

plunder—to steal food, valuables, or other supplies by force.

receipt—a written acknowledgement that payment is due for goods or weapons taken by Patriot forces.

regiment—a military unit commanded by a colonel, consisting of several hundred soldiers divided into smaller battalions and companies.

shoal—an underwater sandbar or sandbank that is visible at low tide.

smallpox—a contagious disease that causes scarring of the skin, blindness, and in some cases, death.

subordinate—someone who is lower in rank or status.

Further Reading

Books for Students:

Bodie, Idella. *The Revolutionary Swamp Fox*. Orangeburg, S.C.: Sandlapper Publishing, 1999.

Cornelius, Kay. *Francis Marion: The Swamp Fox*. Philadelphia: Chelsea House Publishers, 2001.

Grant, Matthew. *Francis Marion: Swamp Fox*. Mankato, Minn.: Creative Education, 1974.

Strum, Richard M. *Causes of the American Revolution*. Stockton, N.J.: OTTN Publishing, 2005.

Towles, Louis P. *Francis Marion: The Swamp Fox of the American Revolution*. New York: PowerPlus Books, 2002.

Books for Older Readers:

Bass, Robert D. *Swamp Fox: The Life and Campaigns of General Francis Marion*. New York: Henry Holt, 1959.

Buchanan, John. *The Road to Guilford Courthouse: The American Revolution in the Carolinas*. New York: John Wiley and Sons, 1997.

Edgar, Walter. *Partisans and Redcoats: The Southern Conflict that Turned the Tide of the American Revolution*. New York: Perennial, 2001.

Middlekauff, Robert. *The Glorious Cause: The American Revolution, 1763–1789*. 2nd edition. New York: Oxford University Press, 2005.

Rankin, Hugh F. *Francis Marion: The Swamp Fox*. New York: Crowell, 1973.

Williams, Beryl, and Samuel Epstein. *Francis Marion, Swamp Fox of the Revolution*. New York: Julian Messner, 1956.

Wood, W. J. *Battles of the Revolutionary War*, 1775–1781. Cambridge, Mass.: Da Capo Press, 2003.

http://www.gwd50.k12.sc.us/FrancisMarion.htm

The place to start for anyone interested in Francis Marion. This site provides links to other sites on the revolutionary war general.

http://www.fmarion.edu/about/1999995947/1999978 686.htm

A short biography of Francis Marion published by Francis Marion University. Includes a bibliography on Marion.

http://www.americanrevolution.com/FrancisMarion.htm

This biography of Francis Marion comes from the web site The American Revolution. This site includes biographies, a time line, and summaries of the major battles.

http://library.fmarion.edu/english/jarl/fm_bib.html

An extensive bibliography of juvenile and adult works on Francis Marion. Published by Rogers Library at Francis Marion University.

http://www.americaslibrary.gov/cgi-bin/page.cgi/jb/ revolut

This Library of Congress website provides information about people and events of the American Revolution.

http://www.usahistory.info/south/war.html

This website provides information about the American Revolution in the South.

Index

Actaeon (British ship), 12–13
American Revolution
    end of the, 67–68
    start of the, 10, 23–24
    See also Great Britain; individual
      battle names
Arnold, Benedict, 33

Ball, John, 42
Battle of Camden, 35, 37
Battle of Cowpens, 53
Battle of Eutaw Springs, 65–67
Battle of Fort Sullivan, 9–14, 25, 27
Battle of King's Mountain, 44
Buchanan, John, 7
Burgoyne, John, 27

Charleston, S.C.
    and the Battle of Fort Sullivan, 9–14,
      27
    founding of, 15
    siege of, 28–31
    See also South Carolina
Cherokee tribe, 18–21
Clinton, Henry, 12, 28, 31
Continental Army, 27, 28, 63–64
    founding of the, 23–24
    in the South, 32–34, 50–51
Continental Congress, 23, 32
Cordes, Esther. *See* Marion, Gabriel and
    Esther (parents)
Cornwallis, Charles, 37, 41, 44–45, 48,
    54, 56–57, 65, 67

Doyle, Welbore, 55–56

Eutaw Springs, 65–67

Ferguson, Patrick, 44
Fort Johnson, 69–70
Fort Motte, 59–62
Fort Sullivan, 9–14, 25, 27
Fort Watson, 57–59
France, 27–28
Fraser, Thomas, 68
French and Indian War, 18–22

Ganey, Micajah, 39–40, 53, 67–68
Gates, Horatio, 6, 27, 32–35, 50–51

George III (King), 22
    See also Great Britain
Georgetown, 54–55, 62, 64
Georgia, 28, *29*
Grant, James, 19–20
Great Britain
    army of, in South Carolina, 28–32,
      35–39, 44–48, 53–67
    and the Battle of Fort Sullivan, 9–14
    and the French and Indian War,
      18–22
    settlements of, in North America, 15
    and the start of the American
      Revolution, 10, 22–24
    surrender of, at Yorktown, 67, *68*
    See also Loyalists
Great White Marsh, 40–42
Greene, Nathanael, 6, 51–52, 56–57,
    59, 62–65, 67, 68
guerrilla tactics, 36–40, 42–43, 44–45,
    50–53, 55, 71
Guilford Courthouse (North Carolina),
    56–57

Horry, Peter, 17, 34, 39, 43, 54, *60,
    61*, 66, 67
Howe, William, 10, 28
Huguenots, 15–16

James, John, 32
James, William, 7, 34

Keegan, John, 7

Lee, Charles, 11, 13
Lee, Henry ("Light Horse Harry"), 6,
    53–54, 56–62, 63, 64, 67, *71*
Lincoln, Benjamin, 30–31
Loyalists, 28, 31–32, 61, 64–65, 69
    1782 uprising, 67–68
    and British taxes, 22
    defeat of, at Charleston, 10
    rebellion of, in South Carolina, 25,
      26–27
    search of, for Marion, 39–45
    See also Great Britain

Maham, Hezekiah, 58–59
maps, 19, 58

Numbers in ***bold italics*** refer to captions.

Picture Credits

Page:

2: US Senate Collection
8: Library of Congress
8-9: US Senate Collection
12: Library of Congress
13: From *The Story of the Revolution* by Henry Cabot Lodge
16: MPI/Getty Images
19: © OTTN Publishing
20: Library of Congress
23: Paintings by Don Troiani, www.historicalartprints.com
26: Library of Congress
29: From *The Story of the Revolution* by Henry Cabot Lodge
30: Independence National Historical Park
31: General Sir Henry Clinton (1730-95) c. 1777 (w/c on ivory) by Smart, John (1741-1811) © Courtesy of the Council, National Army Museum, London, UK/The Bridgeman Art Library
33: Independence National Historical Park
37: Charles, 1st Marquess Cornwallis (1738-1805) (gouache on paper) by Gardner, Daniel (1750-1805)

© Private Collection/The Bridgeman Art Library
38: © North Wind/North Wind Picture Archives
41: US Senate Collection
43: "Marion Crossing the Peede" by William Tylee Ranney, Amon Carter Museum, Fort Worth, Texas
46: Colonel Banastre Tarleton (1754-1833) 1782 (oil on canvas) by Reynolds, Sir Joshua (1723-92) National Gallery, London, UK/The Bridgeman Art Library
49: Library of Congress
52: Independence National Historical Park
54: Independence National Historical Park
58: © OTTN Publishing
60: US Senate Collection
63: Independence National Historical Park
66: From *The Story of the Revolution* by Henry Cabot Lodge
68: Architect of the Capitol
71: Courtesy Burl Kennedy © 2005

Front Cover: Private Collection
Back Cover: US Senate Collection

About the Author

SCOTT KAUFMAN is associate professor of History at Francis Marion University in Florence, South Carolina, where he teaches classes on U.S. History. He is the author of *Confronting Communism: U.S. and British Policies toward China* (University of Missouri Press, 2001), and *The Pig War: The United States, Britain, and the Balance of Power in the Pacific Northwest, 1846-72* (Lexington Books, 2004), and co-author of the revised edition of *The Presidency of James Earl Carter, Jr.* (University Press of Kansas, 2006). He is currently writing a biography of Rosalynn Carter.

Acknowledgements

I would like to thank several people who were kind enough to review and comment on the manuscript: Lindy Thompson, fifth-grade teacher at Briggs Elementary in Florence, South Carolina; Erin Sawyer, second-grade teacher at Pate Elementary in Darlington, South Carolina; Delores Smoot, fifth-grade teacher at Pate Elementary in Darlington; and three of Mrs. Smoot's students, Kayla Hill, Austin Jernigan, and Liam Tindall.

23